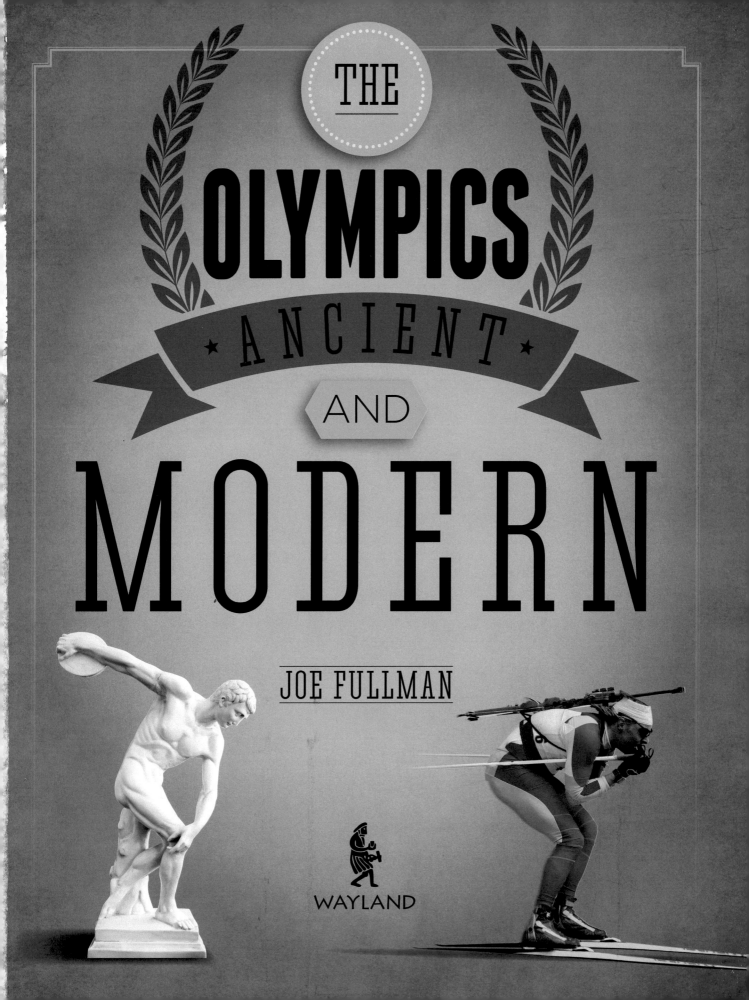

THE OLYMPICS

ANCIENT

AND

MODERN

JOE FULLMAN

WAYLAND

CONTENTS

THE BIGGEST SHOW
ON EARTH

Attracting the world's top athletes and watched by a TV audience of billions, the Winter and Summer Olympics are the biggest sporting shows on Earth. Each competition is followed by the Paralympic Games.

MORE AND MORE

At the first modern Olympics in 1896, there were 43 events in nine sports. At the Summer Olympics in London, 2012, this had grown to 302 events in 26 sports. Another two sports have been added for the Rio de Janeiro Games in 2016: golf and rugby sevens.

Summer Olympic Sports:
Aquatics (including swimming and diving) • Canoeing • Cycling • Gymnastics • Volleyball • Equestrian • Wrestling • Archery • Athletics • Badminton • Basketball • Boxing • Fencing • Field Hockey • Football • Golf • Handball • Judo • Modern Pentathlon • Rowing • Rugby Sevens • Sailing • Shooting • Table Tennis • Taekwondo • Tennis • Triathlon • Weightlifting

The Olympic story began way back in 776 BCE in ancient Greece. For over a thousand years, until 394 CE, a sporting competition was held here every four years. All the best Greek athletes travelled to a religious site called Olympia to compete in a range of sporting events, including races, boxing and wrestling matches, and throwing competitions, such as the discus.

After a break of more than 1,500 years, a modern version of the Olympics was started in 1896 by Baron Pierre de Coubertin (see page 12). It featured many of the ancient Greek sports.

Events at the Winter Olympics include skiing, snowboarding, ice hockey and the bobsleigh (above).

WINTER HOSTS

Since 1924, 19 cities have hosted the Winter Olympics. At the 2014 Winter Games in Sochi, Russia (right), the organizers had to use artificial snow as the venue was too warm for it to occur naturally.

KEY DATES

776 BCE
The first recorded Olympic Games takes place, although there may have been even earlier unrecorded Games.

772 BCE
The second Olympic Games is staged. As with the first, there is just one event, a short foot race called the *stadion*.

748 BCE
For the first time, winners are presented with an olive wreath, known as a *kotinos*, which was cut from a sacred olive tree growing at Olympia.

THE EYES OF THE WORLD

An estimated 4 billion people – or two-thirds of the world's total population – watched some part of the 2012 London Olympics. The Games involved more than 10,000 athletes (compared with just 241 in 1896) from 204 countries (14 in 1896) and were watched live by 7 million spectators.

Events at the 1896 Olympics included running, discus and wrestling, as well as modern sports such as cycling and shooting. Winter sports, such as skiing and skating, were given their own competition, the Winter Olympics, from 1924 onwards. In 1960, a Summer Paralympics was introduced.

SUMMER HOSTS

There have been 25 Summer Olympics held in 22 different cities. Host cities are usually named at least six years in advance to give them time to prepare. In 2012, London (above) became the first city to host three Games, having already staged competitions in 1908 and 1948.

KEY DATES

724 BCE
A second, slightly longer foot race known as the *diaulos*, where athletes have to complete one lap of the track, is introduced.

720 BCE
A third, much longer foot race known as the *dolichos*, and consisting of many laps of the track, is introduced.

708 BCE
More sports are added, including wrestling (*pale*) and the five-event pentathlon.

THE ANCIENT
GAMES

First staged more than 2,700 years ago, the ancient Olympic Games were a religious festival held in honour of Zeus, the king of the Greek gods.

FROM FAR AND WIDE

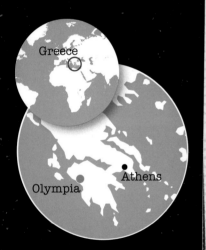

Greece

Olympia   Athens

It wasn't just athletes from Greece who took part in the Olympics. People travelled to Olympia for the Games from as far away as the Greek colonies in Italy and Turkey. At Olympia, around 50,000 people could sit in the main stadium.

The Games were hugely popular and they continued even after Greece became part of the Roman Empire in the second century BCE. However, they were eventually abolished by the Roman emperor Theodosius I in 394 CE. By that time, Rome had converted to Christianity, leading the emperor to ban the festivals of all other religions.

During the first few centuries of the Olympics' existence, Greece was not a single country. Instead, it was a collection of independent lands known as city states.

KEY DATES

708 BCE
Boxing (*pygmachia*) is introduced. Both boxers and wrestlers train at a special area at Olympia called the *palaestra*.

680 BCE
Four-horse chariot racing (*tethrippon*) is held at a special venue at Olympia called the *hippodrome* and the Games are extended to two days.

648 BCE
A violent new sport called *pankration*, involving elements of both boxing and wrestling, is introduced. It is not a modern Olympic sport.

IN THE NUDE

All the competitors at the Olympics were male and competed in the nude. The audience was also made up almost entirely of men, although it is believed that unmarried women were also allowed to attend the Games.

The Greeks considered fire to be sacred, and so kept a flame burning on the altar of Hestia, the goddess of the hearth, throughout the Games. The Games ended with a ceremony where 100 oxen were sacrificed.

OLYMPIC FACTS

The winner of each event had an olive wreath placed on his head – the olive tree was considered sacred in ancient Greece. The most successful athletes became famous celebrities – they had songs written about their feats and statues of them were erected at Olympia.

Greek city states were often at war with each other. While the Games were being held, a 'Sacred Truce' was declared so that athletes and spectators could travel to the Olympic Games in safety.

WONDER OF THE WORLD

In the fifth century BCE, an enormous temple dedicated to Zeus was built at Olympia. Inside was a giant 13-metre tall statue of the god that was later named one of the Seven Wonders of the Ancient World, showing the importance the Greeks placed on the Olympics.

KEY DATES

632 BCE
Olympic events for young boys are staged, including the stadion foot race, wrestling and the pentathlon, and the competition is extended to three days.

520 BCE
The *hoplitodromos* event, in which the athletes have to race in heavy armour, is added to the Olympics.

500 BCE
Although the exact start date is not known, the separate women's competition, the Heraean Games have begun by this time.

EVENTS AT THE ANCIENT
GAMES

The very first Olympic Games in 776 BCE were not the spectacular event they would later become. The competition consisted of just a single race and was over in a day.

The original Olympic sport was a foot race of around 190 metres. It was known as the *stadion*, which was also the name of the earth track where it took place, from where we get the word 'stadium'. Around 20 competitors took part. The winner of the very first *stadion* was a baker called Coroebus from the city of Elis, next to Olympia.

THE RACE OF SOLDIERS

First run in 520 BCE, the *hoplitodromos*, or 'Race of Soldiers' was the only event in which the competitors were not naked. Instead, they ran wearing the heavy helmet, greaves (shin guards), and shield of a Greek soldier (known as a hoplite).

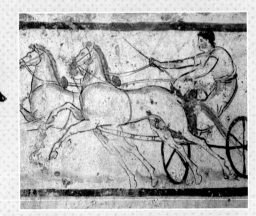

CHARIOT RACING

Olympic chariot races were fast, furious and often very dangerous, with numerous accidents and injuries. They were also a way for wealthy non-athletes to gain Olympic fame, as it was the owner of the chariot, rather than the rider, who was declared the 'victor'.

KEY DATES

472 BCE
The competition is extended to five days, with ceremonies on the first and last days and sporting events held on the middle three.

420 BCE
The Spartans are banned from the Games for performing a military exercise and breaking the 'Sacred Truce'.

408 BCE
A new two-horse chariot race known as the *synoris* is added to the Olympic schedule.

BOXING

There were no rounds in Greek boxing. Fighters fought until one was either knocked out or gave up. There were also no weight classes, so large boxers often fought much smaller ones. Boxers' hands were wrapped in sharp pieces of leather, called *himantes*, which could inflict a lot of damage.

A second race, in which competitors had to complete a lap of the *stadion*, was introduced in 724 BCE, and a third, consisting of several laps, in 720 BCE. Over the next few centuries, more sports were introduced, including boxing, wrestling and *pankration* (a sort of mixture of both), chariot racing, long jump and javelin throwing.

The Olympics featured an artistic competition, attracting many artists, sculptors and poets to Olympia. These artists often made images of the athletes. There was also a competition for the best trumpeter and herald, who introduced the events.

FIVE TIME CHAMPIONS

The pentathlon was perhaps the most challenging event of all. The winner had to master five different sports: discus, javelin, running, wrestling and long jump. For the long jump, athletes held heavy weights in their hands, which they swung forwards as they leapt to help them go farther.

9

KEY DATES

396 BCE
A competition to find the best herald (announcer) and trumpeter is introduced.

392 BCE
The chariot owner Kyniska of Sparta becomes the first woman to win an Olympic olive wreath.

356 BCE
The Macedonian king Philip II wins an Olympic chariot race in the same year that his son, Alexander the Great, is born.

ANCIENT ATHLETES

Training to be an Olympic athlete was hard and intense, but the rewards were worth it. The victors were the superstars of their day with huge followings of fans.

Athletes started training in their home towns 10 months before the Olympics. With a month to go, they moved to Elis, the nearest city to Olympia. Here, they swore an oath to Zeus, confirming they had trained for the full 10 months and promising to obey the competition's rules. Ten judges called *Hellanodikai* oversaw the final month of training and led the athletes from Elis to Olympia for the opening ceremony and the start of the Games.

The *Hellanodikai* enforced the rules during the Games, and

10

KING OF THE SPRINTERS

Leonidas, of the Greek island of Rhodes, was the greatest sprinter of the ancient Olympic Games. Between the ages of 24 and 36, he won three races at four consecutive Olympic Games, gaining a total of 12 Olympic wreaths.

ALL (MEN) WELCOME

Nearly all the sporting events took place in the *stadion*. The athletes entered through an arch, which still stands today (right). All Greek male citizens who weren't slaves could take part in the Olympics. There were no class restrictions, so members of royalty might compete against shepherds. No women were allowed to compete.

KEY DATES

80 BCE
Greece is now part of the Roman Empire. This year's competition is held in Rome, before moving back to Olympia for the next Games.

17 CE
The Roman emperor Tiberius competes in, and wins, the four-horse chariot race.

67 CE
The emperor Nero also proves victorious in the chariot race despite apparently falling from his chariot at one point.

Croton was the home of Astylos. He won several events at the 480 BCE Games, and had a statue of him put up in Croton. However, in 484 BCE, the officials of Syracuse paid for him to represent them instead, so the people of Croton tore down his statue.

OLYMPIC FACTS

Introduced to the Games in 708 BCE, wrestling was the first Olympic event that was not a race. One of the most famous wrestlers was Milo of Croton, who won six consecutive titles between 540–516 BCE. He supposedly gained his enormous strength as a young man by lifting a calf every day until it turned into a bull.

took an oath of their own, promising to judge the competition fairly. They often played an active role in events. For instance, if they thought a boxer wasn't trying hard enough, they might strike him on the back with a stick to make him fight harder.

11

YOU CAN'T TOUCH HIM

Ancient Greek boxing could be a brutal sport, although not when Melankomas of Caria was fighting. He won an Olympic title in 49 BCE, and was said to be so skillful that no other boxer could land a punch on him. He also never threw any punches himself, instead winning by exhausting his opponents.

KEY DATES

261 CE
The final Olympic Games for which the names of the winners have survived take place.

393 CE
The Christian emperor of Rome, Theodosius I, bans all pagan festivals, bringing the Olympic Games to an end.

426 CE
Theodosius II goes even further and orders the destruction of all the temples at Olympia.

THE MODERN
GAMES

More than 1,500 years since the last race was run, the Olympics were brought back into existence in 1896. The first modern Games were also held in Greece, but in the capital, Athens, rather than at Olympia.

By the mid 19th century, interest in the ancient Olympics was growing throughout Europe. In Britain, a small athletic competition based on the Games, called the Wenlock Olympian Games, was held yearly from 1850. And in 1859, 1870 and 1875, a recreation of the Olympics was also staged in Athens, although it was open only to Greek athletes.

DRAWING A CROWD

Between 6–15 April 1896, around 80,000 people a day packed into the rebuilt ancient Panathenaic Stadium in Athens to watch the thrills and spills of the first modern Olympics. This was the largest ever crowd for a sporting event at the time.

BARON PIERRE DE COUBERTIN

The man behind the modern Olympic Games was born into an aristocratic family in 1863. He developed a passionate belief in the power of sport both to improve people's characters and to create peace and understanding between nations.

KEY DATES

1612
Following a revival of interest in ancient Greece, an English barrister stages the 'Cotswold Olympick Games' featuring fencing, horse racing and shin kicking.

1766
Having been buried by flood deposits, the ancient site of Olympia is rediscovered by the English archaeologist Richard Chandler.

1796
The French stage an Olympic-style competition, L'Olympiad de la République, in 1796 and 1798.

Unlike the ancient Games, the modern Olympics have always moved from city to city. They begin and end with spectacular opening and closing ceremonies. These feature speeches, a parade by the athletes and an 'Artistic Program' of singing, dancing and music.

13

These events gave a French educator called Pierre de Coubertin the idea of staging a full-scale, modern version of the Olympics that would bring together athletes from different countries. He established the International Olympic Committee (IOC) in 1894 to help him realize his dreams. Two years later, the first Games of the modern Olympics took place. The IOC still organizes the Games today.

LAKE PLACID 1980

BIATHLON 20km. АНАТОЛИЙ АЛЯБЬЕВ

GOLD, SILVER AND BRONZE

In 1896, the winners received a silver medal, while the runners up were given copper ones. This system was changed at the 1904 Olympics. Since then, the first-place athlete has received a gold medal, the second-placed athlete a silver medal, and the third-placed athlete a bronze medal.

KEY DATES

1850
A yearly Olympic-style competition is begun in Much Wenlock, UK, and is later attended by the French aristocrat Baron Pierre de Coubertin.

1859
The Greek businessman Evangelis Zappas sponsors the Zappas Olympics for Greek athletes in 1859, 1870 and 1875.

1894
Having decided to try and create a new international version of the Olympics, Coubertin founds the International Olympic Committee.

GROWTH OF THE
GAMES

Following the huge success of Athens in 1896, the next two Olympics in Paris, France, and St Louis, USA, weren't as successful. But the Games' popularity soon began to grow.

LORD OF THE RINGS

First shown at the 1920 Games, the official symbol of the Olympics shows five interlocking coloured rings. Designed by the Games' founder, Pierre de Coubertin, the rings are supposed to represent the five regions of the world coming together.

The 1900 and 1904 Olympics were held as part of World Fairs and were rather overshadowed by the cultural exhibitions. The Games held in London in 1908 were more successful. Lasting for 187 days, it's still the longest Olympic event ever held. After 1912, the Games were postponed for World War I and not staged again until 1920.

THE OLYMPIC TORCH RELAY

The tradition of the torch relay began at the 1936 Berlin Games. Several months before the Games, a torch is lit at the temple of Hera in Olympia using sunlight reflected by a mirror. The torch then travels via a relay of runners to the host city where it is used to light the Olympic flame.

KEY DATES

1896 ATHENS, GREECE
The first modern Olympics is staged in the Panathenaic Stadium. The winners receive a silver medal and an olive branch.

1900 PARIS, FRANCE
There is no stadium for the second Olympics. Instead, running events are held in a park, and swimming events in the River Seine.

1904 ST LOUIS, USA
The third Olympic Games forms part of a more general World's Fair and is the first to feature gold, silver and bronze medals.

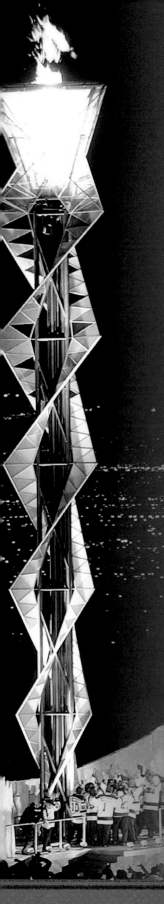

OLYMPIC FLAME

In 1928 in Amsterdam, the idea of having an Olympic flame, which used to burn at the ancient Olympics, was revived. At every Games since, a flame has been lit at a purpose-built cauldron in the Olympic Stadium and kept burning throughout the entire competition.

In the 1920s and 30s, the Olympics really began to grow in status. Many of the Games' best-known features were introduced in this period, including the Olympic flag, the torch relay and the lighting of the Olympic flame. The Games were brought to a halt again by World War II, but since they restarted at London in 1948, they've been held every four years and have become the most-watched sporting event in the world.

OLYMPIC OATH

The Games in 1920 saw the introduction of an Olympic oath, which read:

"We swear we will take part in the Olympic Games in a spirit of chivalry, for the honour of our country and for the glory of sport."

This has since been changed to:

"In the name of all the competitors, I promise that we shall take part in these Olympic Games, respecting and abiding by the rules which govern them, committing ourselves to a sport without doping and without drugs, in the true spirit of sportsmanship, for the glory of sport and the honour of our teams."

15

AMATEUR VERSUS PROFESSIONAL

To begin with, all Olympic athletes had to be amateurs. Indeed Jim Thorpe (right), who won the pentathlon and decathlon for the USA at the 1912 Games, was stripped of his medals when it was discovered that he had been paid to play baseball in the past. In the 1980s, the rules were relaxed and now nearly all Olympic athletes are professionals.

KEY DATES

1908 LONDON, UK
This is the first Olympic Games to be staged in a purpose-built stadium. The first winter sport, figure skating, is introduced.

1912 STOCKHOLM, SWEDEN
For the first time, athletes from all five continents compete at the Olympic Games.

1916 BERLIN, GERMANY
The Games due to be held in Berlin are cancelled because of World War I.

THE WINTER
OLYMPICS

In 1921, the IOC decided to create a new competition that would feature winter sports, such as skiing, skating and ice hockey. The first Winter Olympics were held in Chamonix, France in 1924.

THE SPORTS OF THE WINTER OLYMPICS

The Winter Olympics involves 98 events in 15 sports:

Alpine Skiing • Biathlon • Bobsleigh • Cross Country Skiing • Curling • Figure Skating • Freestyle Skiing • Ice Hockey • Luge • Nordic Combined • Short Track Speed Skating • Skeleton • Ski Jumping • Snowboarding • Speed Skating

Indoor winter sports, such as ice skating, were staged at the first few Olympic Games. However, as the Games were staged in summer, outdoor winter sports couldn't be featured. The decision to establish a separate Winter Olympics solved this problem. At the first Games, competitors took part in five sports: bobsleigh, curling, ice hockey, skiing (including cross country and ski jumping, but not downhill skiing) and skating. Several more sports were added at subsequent Games, including Alpine (downhill) skiing, speed skating and snowboarding.

KEY DATES

1920 ANTWERP, BELGIUM
The defeated powers of Germany, Austria and Turkey are banned from taking part in the first Games after World War I.

1924 PARIS & CHAMONIX, FRANCE
France hosts both its second Summer Games in Paris and its first Winter Games in Chamonix.

1928 ST MORITZ, SWITZERLAND
Warm temperatures lead to the cancellation of some events at the second Winter Olympics.

OLDEST AND YOUNGEST

The oldest Winter Olympics winner was a 54-year-old Briton, Robin Welsh. He won the gold in curling in 1924, a game played on ice where players slide rounded stones into a circular target. The youngest winner was a 13-year-old South Korean, Yun-Mi Kim, who won the gold in speed skating in 1994.

Biathlon, a combination of skiing and shooting, is one of the most distinctive winter sports. There are several races, all of which involve competitors skiing for a certain distance and then shooting at five targets before repeating the process.

So far, 11 nations, all in the Northern Hemisphere, have hosted the Winter Olympics. To begin with, the Winter Games were held in the same year as the Summer Olympics. After 1992, however, it was decided to stage the Games two years apart so that each received the maximum attention.

TOP WINTER COUNTRIES

NORWAY
329 MEDALS

USA
281 MEDALS

AUSTRIA
218 MEDALS

Unsurprisingly, it is those countries with the coldest climates and plenty of snow and ice where athletes can practise that top the medal charts. Norway has won the most medals with 329, including 118 golds, with the USA in second place with 281 medals, and Austria in third with 218 medals.

KEY DATES

1928 AMSTERDAM, NETHERLANDS
For the first time, the Olympic flame is lit and kept burning throughout the competition.

1932 USA
At the Summer Olympics in Los Angeles, winning athletes stand on a tiered platform with the national flags raised above them. The USA also hosts the Winter Olympics at Lake Placid.

1936 GERMANY
The Berlin Summer Olympics is the first to be televised, while the Winter Olympics in Garmisch-Partenkirchen is the first to feature Alpine skiing.

THE PARALYMPICS

The Paralympic Games for athletes with disabilities are staged immediately after each Summer and Winter Olympics at the same venues. These Games are now a major international sporting competition.

The first official competition for athletes with an impairment was held at the 1948 Olympics. A German neurologist, Dr Ludwigg Guttman, organized a competition for war veterans at Stoke Mandeville hospital in England. Sixteen men and women took part in an archery competition. The Games were held again four years later when the involvement of Dutch competitors turned it into an international event.

SPORTS

There are 24 sports contested at the Summer Paralympics, and five at the Winter Paralympics.

Summer Sports:
Archery • Athletics • Badminton • Boccia • Canoeing • Cycling • Equestrian • 5-a-side Football • Goalball • Judo • Powerlifting • Rowing • Sailing • Shooting • Sitting Volleyball • Swimming • Table Tennis • Triathlon • Wheelchair Basketball • Wheelchair Dance Sport • Wheelchair Fencing • Wheelchair Rugby • Wheelchair Tennis

Winter Sports:
Alpine Skiing • Biathlon • Cross-Country Skiing • Ice Sledge Hockey • Wheelchair Curling

THE FIRST PARALYMPIAN

The first athlete to compete in the Olympics with a disability was the American gymnast, George Eyser in 1904. He had an artificial leg but still managed to win three golds, two silvers and one bronze.

KEY DATES

1940 & 1944
Both of these Games are cancelled because of World War II.

1948 St Moritz, Switzerland
The defeated nations, Germany and Japan, are not invited to take part in the first Winter Olympics after World War II.

1948 London, UK
London's second Olympics coincides with a small competition for disabled athletes held just outside London, which goes on to become the Paralympic Games.

MOST DECORATED ATHLETE

The American Trischa Zorn is the most successful Paralympian of all time.

5 BRONZE

9 SILVER

41 GOLD

She competed in the blind swimming competition in seven consecutive Games from 1980 to 2004, winning a total of 55 medals.

The British Games grew to become the Paralympics, which was first staged in Rome in 1960 when 400 athletes from 23 countries took part. At first, only wheelchair-bound athletes could compete. From 1976 onwards, athletes with other impairments were welcomed, including amputees and those who were visually impaired.

NEW SPORTS

There are two Paralympic sports that don't feature in the Olympics. The first is boccia (left), which is a bit like bowls or petanque. The second is goalball, in which visually impaired players must use their hearing to detect, catch and pass a ball with bells in it to score goals.

KEY DATES

1952 OSLO, NORWAY, AND HELSINKI, FINLAND
Germany and Japan are finally invited to compete at the Winter Games in Oslo, and the Summer Games in Helsinki.

1956 CORTINA D'AMPEZZO, ITALY
Warm temperatures result in snow having to be imported so Italy's first Winter Olympics can be staged.

1956 MELBOURNE, AUSTRALIA
Political conflicts mean that several countries boycott the first southern hemisphere Games, including Egypt, the Netherlands, Spain and China.

TROUBLED
GAMES

The Olympics' founder saw the Games as a way of bringing nations together, and promoting good sportsmanship. But some nations have used the Games for political ends, while a few athletes have cheated.

BOYCOTTS

Several African nations refused to participate in the 1976 Games in Montreal. They were protesting against the presence of New Zealand, whose rugby team had toured South Africa, where the racist Apartheid government was in charge.

MUNICH TRAGEDY

The Olympic Games have often been used as a stage by political groups wanting to attract attention. Munich in 1972 was the venue for the Olympics' darkest hour when 11 Israeli athletes were killed by the Palestinian terrorist group Black September as a protest against Israel's government.

One of the most controversial Olympic Games was staged in Berlin in 1936 by Adolf Hitler's Nazi regime. Hitler thought the Games would provide an international stage on which to prove the superiority of Germans. The Nazis spent a vast sum of money building the then-biggest sports stadium in the world so that 110,000 spectators could watch the country's triumph.

The Nazi regime brutally persecuted people of other races whom they considered to be

In 1980 and 1984, the USA and the Soviet Union engaged in tit-for-tat boycotts. The USA boycotted the 1980 Moscow Games as a protest against the Soviet invasion of Afghanistan. The Soviets then boycotted the Los Angeles Games.

KEY DATES

1960 SQUAW VALLEY, USA
Walt Disney organizes the opening and closing ceremonies of the Winter Games, which are held in a sports resort, rather than a city.

1960 ROME, ITALY
Rome hosts its first Summer Games as well as the first official Paralympic Games.

1964 INNSBRUCK, AUSTRIA
Huge amounts of snow and ice have to be brought from a mountain top to Innsbruck by the Austrian army so the Winter Games can go ahead.

PRESSING BUTTONS

Some cheats have relied not on drugs but on technology. At the 1976 Olympics, the Soviet fencer Boris Onischenko added a button to his épée (sword) which would automatically score a hit even if he hadn't touched his opponent. It was discovered and he was thrown out of the competition.

inferior. Their theories were destroyed when African American sprinter Jesse Owens won four gold medals at the Games in the 100m, 200m, long jump and 4 x 100m relay.

DRUG CHEATS

Over the years, some athletes have tried to cheat, usually by taking performance-enhancing drugs. A number of sprinters have been revealed to be drugs cheats including Ben Johnson, the winner of the 1988 men's 100m and Marion Jones (above left) who won the women's 100m, 200m, Long Jump, 4 x 100m and 4 x 400m at Sydney in 2000.

KEY DATES

1964 TOKYO, JAPAN
The Summer Games are the first held in Asia and the first to be broadcast live via satellite.

1968 GRENOBLE, FRANCE
The Winter Games are the first to feature both a mascot (Schuss the Skier) and drug testing.

1968 MEXICO CITY, MEXICO
The Games are held at 2,240m above sea level, the highest ever. The thin air at this altitude leads to many record-breaking performances.

WOMEN AND THE
OLYMPICS

The road to Olympic glory has been much longer for women than men. Women could not take part at all in the ancient Olympics. Only recently have they been able to compete on an equal footing.

THE FIRST FEMALE CHAMPION

Married women could neither take part in nor watch the ancient Games. However there was still a way for them to get involved. As the owner of the winning chariots at the 396 BCE and 392 BCE Olympics, Kyniska, daughter of the king of Sparta, was presented with the victory wreaths, making her the first female winner at the Olympic Games.

The ancient Olympics were a male-only affair. However, in the sixth century BCE, a competition for women known as the Heraean Games was established at Olympia in honour of the goddess Hera. As with the Olympics, it started out as a series of foot races before other events, such as chariot races, were added. Women did not compete in the nude, but in men's clothing, and men were allowed to watch.

Women first competed at the Olympics in 1900, but only in a handful of events: tennis, sailing, croquet, horseriding and golf.

KEY DATES

1972 SAPPORO, JAPAN
Sapporo, which would have staged the 1940 Games had it not been for World War II, hosts Asia's first Winter Games.

1972 MUNICH, GERMANY
The sporting competition of the Summer Games is overshadowed by the murder of 11 Israeli athletes by the Black September Terrorist Group.

1976 INNSBRUCK, AUSTRIA
Innsbruck hosts its second Winter Olympics in 12 years when the original host city, Denver, pulls out over the cost of the Games.

WOMEN ONLY

There are now a couple of Olympic sports in which only women compete: rhythmic gymnastics and synchronized swimming. There are also two sports in which men and women compete directly against one another: sailing and horseriding.

Gradually more events were added, but it would not be until 1928 that women were allowed to take part in athletic competitions. At those Games, women were not allowed to run any distance longer than 800m. Of the field events, women only competed in the high jump and the discus.

Today almost as many women take part in the Olympics as men. At the 1900 Olympics, only 22 out 997 athletes were women, or just over 2 per cent. This had risen to 4,776 out of 10,700 (44 per cent) by the Summer Games in London 2012.

SLOWLY DOES IT

Events for women have been slowly added to the Olympic programme over the past century, although often in a restricted form. For instance, the first women's marathon wasn't held until 1984 and the first women's ski jumping competition wasn't staged until 2014.

Timeline of Women's Sports at the Olympics

Year	Sport
1900	Golf, Tennis (Tennis dropped after 1924 Games, reinstated in 1988)
1904	Archery
1908	Figure Skating
1912	Swimming
1924	Fencing
1928	Gymnastics, Athletics
1936	Alpine Skiing
1948	Canoeing
1952	Equestrian Sports
1960	Speed Skating
1964	Volleyball, Luge
1976	Rowing, Basketball, Handball
1980	Field Hockey
1984	Shooting, Cycling
1988	Table Tennis, Sailing
1992	Badminton, Judo, Biathlon
1996	Football, Softball
1998	Curling, Ice Hockey
2000	Weightlifting, Pentathlon, Taekwondo, Triathlon
2002	Bobsleigh
2004	Wrestling
2008	BMX
2012	Boxing
2014	Ski Jumping

KEY DATES

1976 MONTREAL, CANADA
The cost of staging the Summer Olympics puts the city heavily in debt, while 31 nations boycott the Games for political reasons.

1980 LAKE PLACID, USA
This is the second time Lake Placid has hosted the Winter Olympics after the Games of 1932.

1980 MOSCOW, USSR
Some 61 nations, including the USA, refuse to participate in the Summer Games as a protest over the Soviets' invasion of Afghanistan the year before.

GREAT
OLYMPIANS

As one of the world's most watched TV events, the Olympics has turned many athletes, from a variety of different sports, into global superstars. These pages look at some of the greatest Olympians.

Name: Aladár Gerevich
Country: Hungary
Dates: 16 Mar 1910–14 May 1991 (81)
Sport: Fencing
Olympic Games: 1932 Los Angeles, 1936 Berlin, 1948 London, 1952 Helsinki, 1956 Melbourne, 1960 Rome
Medals: 10 (7 gold, 1 silver, 2 bronze)

Notes: The greatest fencer of all time, Gerevich won his first gold medal in 1932 aged 22, and his last 28 years later, aged 50. He won golds in six different Olympics.

Name: Birgit Fischer
Country: Germany
Dates: 25 Feb 1962–
Sport: Canoeing
Olympic Games: 1980 Moscow, 1988 Seoul, 1992 Barcelona, 1996 Atlanta, 2000 Sydney, 2004 Athens
Medals: 12 (8 gold, 4 silver)

Notes: Like Gerevich, Fischer won gold at six Olympics, from 1980 to 2004. She won medals in the K-1, K-2 and K-4 500m races, competing for East Germany until 1988, and Germany from 1992.

Name: Chris Hoy
Country: UK
Dates: 23 March 1976–
Sport: Cycling
Olympic Games: 2000 Sydney, 2004 Athens, 2008 Beijing, 2012 London
Medals: 7 (6 gold, 1 silver)

Notes: Hoy is the most successful Olympic cyclist ever. A power sprinter, he won the first of his six gold medals in 2004 in the kilo, a 1-km time trial. Later wins came in both individual and team events.

Name: Emile Zapotek
Country: Czech Republic
Dates: 19 Sep 1922–22 Nov 2000 (78)
Sport: Athletics
Olympic Games: 1948 London, 1952 Helsinki
Medals: 5 (4 gold, 1 silver)

Notes: Zapotek won the three longest races at the 1952 Helsinki Games: the 5,000m, the 10,000m and the marathon. The marathon was the first he'd ever run, entering the event at the last minute.

KEY DATES

1984 SARAJEVO, YUGOSLAVIA
At the first Winter Olympics held in a communist state, the Olympic flag is mistakenly raised upside down during the opening ceremony.

1984 LOS ANGELES, USA
Fifteen communist countries, including the Soviet Union, refuse to participate in the Summer Games in retaliation against the boycott of Moscow.

1988 CALGARY, CANADA
Canada's second Olympics, and its first Winter Games, are the first in which athletes no longer have to be amateurs, following a 1986 ruling by the IOC.

Name: Michael Phelps
Country: USA
Dates: 30 June 1985–
Sport: Swimming
Olympic Games: 2004 Athens, 2008 Beijing, 2012 London
Medals: 22 (18 gold, 2 silver, 2 bronze)

Notes: A specialist in butterfly and freestyle, Phelps holds the record for both the highest number of Summer Olympic medals (22) and the greatest number of golds (18).

MASCOTS

Every Olympics since 1966 has had its own mascot (or mascots), a cartoon character designed to appeal to children. The mascots usually take the form of one of the animals of the host country.

25

Name: Usain Bolt
Country: Jamaica
Dates: 21 Aug 1986–
Sport: Athletics
Olympic Games: 2008 Beijing, 2012 London
Medals: 6 (6 gold)

Notes: The fastest man ever, Bolt set world records at the 100m, 200m and 4 x 100m relay at the 2008 Olympics. In 2012, he became the first person to defend all three sprint titles.

Name: Nadia Comaneci
Country: Romania
Dates: 12 Nov 1961–
Sport: Gymnastics
Olympic Games: 1976 Montreal, 1980 Moscow
Medals: 9 (5 gold, 3 silver, 1 bronze)

Notes: The Romanian was first athlete to be awarded a perfect 10 in an Olympic gymnastics competition for her routine on the uneven bars. She won her first gold at 14 and retired at 19.

Name: Ole Einar Bjørndalen
Country: Norway
Dates: 27 Jan 1974–
Sport: Biathlon
Olympic Games: Lillehammer 1994, Nagano 1998, Salt Lake City 2002, Turin 2006, Vancouver 2010, Sochi 2014
Medals: 13 (8 gold, 4 silver, 1 bronze)

Notes: Bjørndalen is the most successful winter Olympian of all time, winning 13 medals, including 8 golds between 1994 and 2014, by which time he was 40. He is known as the 'King of Biathlon'.

KEY DATES

1988 SEOUL, SOUTH KOREA
The Summer Games become infamous when 11 athletes fail drug tests, including the men's 100m champion, Ben Johnson.

1992 ALBERTVILLE, FRANCE
The venue for France's third Winter Games, and its fifth Games in total, is the smallest place ever to host an Olympics.

1992 BARCELONA, SPAIN
Following the collapse of the Soviet Union, the former Soviet nations compete in the Summer Games as a Unified Team.

RECENT
SUCCESSES

In the 21st century, the Olympic Games have gone from strength to strength. The Games' official motto is *Citius, Altius, Fortius* ('Faster, Higher, Stronger'), and every Olympics tries to become the 'best games ever'.

2002 WINTER OLYMPICS
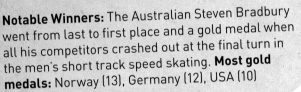

Host City: Salt Lake City, USA – This marked the eighth time the USA had hosted an Olympic competition, more than any other nation.
Motto: Light the Fire Within
No. Athletes: 2399

Notable Winners: The Australian Steven Bradbury went from last to first place and a gold medal when all his competitors crashed out at the final turn in the men's short track speed skating. **Most gold medals:** Norway (13), Germany (12), USA (10)

2000 SUMMER OLYMPICS

Host City: Sydney, Australia – This was the second Summer Games staged in the southern hemisphere and the second one in Australia, after Melbourne in 1956.
Motto: Share the Spirit

No. Athletes: 10,651

Notable Winners: Félix Savón (Cuba) won boxing gold at his third Games. **Most gold medals:** USA (37), Russia (32), China (28)

2004 SUMMER OLYMPICS

Host City: Athens, Greece – The Olympic Games returned to the country of their birth, 108 years after they were last staged there.
Motto: Welcome Home

No. Athletes: 10,625

Notable Winners: Yumileidi Cumbá (Cuba) won the shot put in Olympia at the site of the ancient Olympics, the first time women had officially competed there. **Most gold medals:** USA (36), China (32), Russia (28)

KEY DATES

1994 LILLEHAMMER, NORWAY
Norway's second Winter Games, after 1952 in Oslo, is the first not to be held in the same year as the Summer Games.

1996, ATLANTA, USA
Twenty-four countries compete in the Summer Games for the first time, including several former Soviet countries.

1998 NAGANO, JAPAN
Japan's second Winter Games, and third Games in total, hosts the first ever women's ice hockey competition.

2006 WINTER OLYMPICS

Host City: Turin – These were the third Olympics to be staged in Italy after the Winter Games in Cortina d'Ampezzo in 1956 and the Summer Games in Rome, 1960.

Motto: Passion Lives Here
No. Athletes: 2508

Notable Winners: Italy won their fifth gold medal in the Men's 10km Cross Country Skiing Relay. **Most gold medals:** Germany (11), USA (9), Austria (9)

2008 SUMMER OLYMPICS

Host City: Beijing, China – The third Asian city to host the Olympics, Beijing spared no expense, building 12 brand new venues.
Motto: One World, One Dream
No. Athletes: 10,942

Notable Winners: Eighty-six countries won a medal at the Beijing Olympics, more than at any previous games. Forty-three world records were broken.
Most Gold Medals: China (51), USA (36), Russia (23)

2010 WINTER OLYMPICS

Host City: Vancouver, Canada – These were the third Canadian Olympics after the Summer Games in Montreal, 1976, and the Winter Games in Calgary, 1988.
Motto: With Glowing Hearts
No. Athletes: 2566

Notable Winners: China won all three women's short track skating events: 500m, 1000m and 3000m relay. **Most Gold Medals:** Canada (14), Germany (10), USA (9)

27

2012 SUMMER OLYMPICS

Host City: London, UK – London became the first city to host the Games three times after the Olympics of 1908 and 1948.
Motto: Inspire a Generation
No. Athletes: 10,700

Notable Winners: Misty May-Treanor and Kerri Walsh won their third successive beach volleyball gold. For the first time Jamaican sprinters took the first three positions in the men's 200m. **Most Gold Medals:** USA (46), China (38), UK (29)

2014 WINTER OLYMPICS

Host City: Sochi, Russia – This was the warmest city ever to host a Winter Olympics, forcing it to rely on imported snow.
Motto: Hot. Cool. Yours
No. Athletes: 2873

Notable Winners: The women's downhill was the first Olympic skiing event to end in a tie as Tina Maze of Slovenia and Dominique Gisin of Switzerland both recorded times of 1:41.57. They shared the gold medal. **Most Gold Medals:** Russia (13), Norway (11), Canada (10)

KEY DATES

2000 SYDNEY, AUSTRALIA
Australia's second Summer Games sees British rower Sir Steven Redgrave win his fifth consecutive gold medal.

2002 SALT LAKE CITY, USA
The USA's fourth Winter Games, and eighth Games in total, causes controversy as it is discovered that bribes had been paid in the bidding process.

2004 ATHENS, GREECE
Greece hosts its second Summer Games, but construction problems mean that many of its facilities are completed only just in time.

PLANNING THE
GAMES

Hosting the Olympics is a good way for a city to make a mark on the international stage, but it can come at a price. The cost of hosting the Games has skyrocketed over the years.

Cities compete with each other for the right to host the Olympics. The bidding process alone can cost many millions of dollars. Once chosen, the new Olympic city must finance the Games' entire cost. The IOC does not contribute financially. Its role is to oversee preparations and make sure the facilities are up to standard.

Staging the Olympics can provide a city with a major economic boost, but it can also cause severe financial difficulties. Montreal didn't pay off its Olympic debt until 2006, 30 years after its games. Its Olympic stadium, shown here, was nicknamed 'The Big Owe'.

OLYMPIC PARKS

Most cities create a special Olympic Park where many of the main venues are situated, such as this one in Munich, which served the 1972 Games. Cities often use the construction of an Olympic Park as a way of redeveloping a rundown or poor part of the city.

KEY DATES

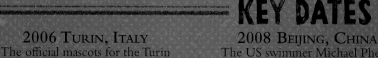

2006 TURIN, ITALY
The official mascots for the Turin Winter Games are Neve, a female snowball, and Glitz, a male ice cube. A record 80 nations take part.

2008 BEIJING, CHINA
The US swimmer Michael Phelps becomes the first person to win eight gold medals at a single Olympics at China's Summer Games.

2010 VANCOUVER, CANADA
Canada sets the record for the number of gold medals won by a nation at the Winter Olympics with 14.

BILLION DOLLAR BUSINESS

The cost of staging the Olympic Games has risen enormously over the years:

Total estimated costs of recent Olympics (including Games-related infrastructure):

| 1948 LONDON £762,000 | 1968 MEXICO CITY $176 MILLION | 1988 SEOUL $4 BILLION | 2008 BEIJING $44 BILLION | 2014 SOCHI $51 BILLION |

There may be some existing sporting facilities that the city can use, but it will also probably have to build several new Olympic-standard venues. For the Summer Olympics, these can include an aquatics centre, an athletics stadium and a basketball arena, while the Winter Olympics might require a new ice hockey rink, curling centre and ski complex. The city also needs to build an athletes' village where the competitors can stay.

WHITE ELEPHANTS

Some host cities have been left with expensive sporting facilities they no longer need once the games are over. Many of the venues created for the Athens games of 2004, such as this swimming centre, were abandoned. The Olympic Park in Sydney remained unused for several years after the games.

KEY DATES

2012 LONDON, UK
The only UK city to have hosted an Olympics, London stages the 20th Summer Games and the 14th Paralympic Games.

2014 SOCHI, RUSSIA
The second Russian city to host an Olympics, after Moscow in 1980, Sochi's Games are the most expensive in history.

2016 RIO DE JANEIRO, BRAZIL
Brazil hosts its first Summer Games just two years after hosting the football World Cup in 2014.

GLOSSARY

ALPINE SKIING
A sport in which competitors use gravity to move them down a skiing course. It's also known as downhill skiiing.

AMATEUR
Someone who is not paid to do a job or take part in an activity or sport.

BOYCOTT
To withdraw from an event, usually as a political protest.

CEREMONY
A formal public event, often involving several carefully planned procedures, staged to celebrate a particular occasion.

CROSS-COUNTRY SKIING
A sport in which competitors use their own power to move them over a flat (or largely flat) skiing course.

HOST CITY
Where an Olympic Games is staged.

INFRASTRUCTURE
The basic structures and facilities that make up an area, such as a city or an Olympic park.

IOC
The International Olympic Committee, the body that organises the Games.

MASCOT
A fictional character, usually in the form of an animal, used to represent or market an event.

MOTTO
A short phrase that is supposed to represent the beliefs or ideals of a person, event or organisation.

OATH
A promise, usually made by an individual (or a group) about their future actions or behaviour.

OLYMPIA
A religious site in ancient Greece where the Olympics were held.

PARALYMPICS
An international sporting competition for athletes with physical disabilities that takes place immediately after the Summer and Winter Olympics.

PROFESSIONAL
Someone who does a job or takes part in an activity or sport for money.

SACRED TRUCE
A period of peace before and during the Ancient Olympics when the Greek city states halted any wars to allow athletes to travel to the games safely.

STADIUM

A circular, or oval-shaped, sports ground surrounded by seating for spectators. It comes from the Ancient Greek word *Stadion*, which was the name of the first Olympic race (and the earth track where it was run).

SUMMER OLYMPICS

An international sporting competition held every four years, featuring a range of athletic, swimming and team sports.

TORCH RELAY

The way in which a series of runners carrying torches transfers the Olympic flame from Olympia to the site of the Olympics. Each runner lights the torch of the next runner.

WINTER OLYMPICS

An international sporting competition held every four years, featuring only winter sports.

WORLD FAIR

A large public cultural exhibition that attracts exhibitors from all over the world. The second and third Olympic Games, in 1900 and 1904, were staged as part of World Fairs.

WEBSITES

www.olympic.org
The official IOC website is packed full of features, statistics and news.

www.rio2016.com/en/the-games/olympic
Website dedicated to the 31st Summer Olympic Games in Rio de Janeiro, Brazil.

www.facebook.com/olympics
Videos, links and constant updates from the IOC's Facebook page.

www.activityvillage.co.uk/olympic-games
Olympic-themed games, puzzles, crafts, activities and worksheets from this great child-orientated website.

INDEX

32

ACKNOWLEDGEMENTS

First published in Great Britain in 2015 by Wayland

Copyright © Wayland, 2015

All rights reserved

Series editor: Elizabeth Brent

Produced by Tall Tree Ltd
Editor: Jon Richards
Designer: Gary Hyde, Ed Simkins, Jonathan Vipond

Dewey number: 796.4'8'09-dc23

ISBN: 978 0 7502 9547 5

FSC

Wayland, an imprint of Hachette Children's Group

Part of Hodder and Stoughton Carmelite House, 50 Victoria Embankment, London EC4Y 0DZ

An Hachette UK Company
www.hachette.co.uk
www.hachettechildrens.co.uk

Printed and bound in China

10 9 8 7 6 5 4 3 2 1

Picture acknowledgements:
Every attempt has been made to clear copyright. Should there be any inadvertent omission, please apply to the publisher for rectification.

The website addresses (URLs) included in this book were valid at the time of going to press. However, it is possible that contents or addresses may have changed since the publication of this book. No responsibility for any such changes can be accepted by either the author or the Publisher.

The publisher would like to thank the following for their kind permission to reproduce their photographs:

Key: t-top, b-bottom, c-centre, l-left, r-right

All images are iStock.com unless otherwise stated.

Front Cover tl public domain, tr Bundeswehr-Fotos, bl Shutterstock.com, br Dreamstime.com. Back Cover Darren Wilkinson. End Papers Dreamstime.com. p6 tl Dreamstime.com, p2 bl Marie-Lan Nguyen, p2–3 c Darren Wilkinson, p3 br UK Department for Culture, Media and Sport, p5 c Dreamstime.com, p5 t Getty Images Mike Hewitt, p6–7 c Dreamstime.com, p7 t Marie-Lan Nguyen, p8 l Marie-Lan Nguyen, p9 tr Matthias Kabel, p9 br Carole Raddato,

p11 br Marie-Lan Nguyen, p13 t Matt Lancashire, p13 br Sergeev Pavel, p14 bl Waerfelu, p18–19 c Shizhao, p19 br Stig Morten Skjæran, p21 br Tomás Galindo, p22 l Wonderlane, pp22–23 c Aurelien Guichard, p23 tr Korea.net / Korean Culture and Information Service (Korean Olympic Committee), p24 tr Getty Images Darren England / Allsport, p24 bl Mark Harkin, p24 br Roger & Renate Rössing, p25 tl Karen Blaha, p25 c PhotoBobil, p25 tr Damien D, p25 cr Augustas Didžgalvis, p25 bl Dave Gilbert, p25 br Tor Atle Kleven, p26 cl Jimmy Harris, p26 br Alterego, p27 bl UK Department for Culture, Media and Sport, pp28–29 c Alain Carpentier, p29 b Tilemahos Efthimiadis, p31 Shizhao.